A CULINARY JOURNEY

Exploring destinations and discovering different cultures and traditions is at the heart of every Viking journey. And of course food – not only the recipes prepared by our onboard chefs, but also local cuisine in all the fascinating places our ships visit – is an essential part of the overall Viking experience.

We hope this book helps you to recreate the flavors of your travels back home in your own kitchen, and inspires you to continue exploring the world.

SOUTHERN EUROPE & NORTH AFRICA

From the vineyards of Italy to the olive groves of Greece and lush valleys of Portugal's Douro River, cuisine from this part of the world is as diverse as the countries themselves. Historically, the Romans had a huge influence on the development of European cuisine, and during the Middle Ages and Renaissance, meat became the central part of the meal. European cuisine then developed in the royal and noble courts, and in the 18th and 19th centuries 'cuisine classique', a mix of aristocratic and French bourgeois cuisine, became the culinary standard in Europe. Wine and dairy products are often used in cooking, and curing, pickling and salting of foods is common. In Egypt, pulses and beans are commonly used as a source of protein as many dishes are vegetarian.

ITALY

From the sun-soaked vineyards of Tuscany to the beautiful Amalfi Coast, Italy offers a rich culinary journey. Each region has its own specialty – the best pizza, for example, is found in Naples; Venice boasts exquisite risotto, while the spaghetti in Rome is a must-try.

SPAGHETTI ALLE VONGOLE

Serves 4

1 lb (450g) fresh clams
2 tbsp olive oil
1 clove garlic
1 tsp red chili, finely
  chopped
2 fl oz (60ml) white
  wine
1 tsp salt
Pinch pepper
1 lb (450g) dried
  spaghetti

TO GARNISH:
Fresh parsley

1 Bring a large pot of salted water to the boil.
Add the spaghetti and cook according to the
pack instructions, stirring occasionally, until the
pasta is just *al dente*.
2 To a cold saucepan, add the olive oil, garlic
and chili. Heat gently until the garlic is just
golden. Add the clams and pour in the wine.
Season with salt and pepper. Cover and cook
over a medium heat for 3 to 4 minutes, shaking
the pan occasionally.
3 Drain the pasta and transfer to a large bowl.
Add the clams, including all the pan juices, and
toss well. Discard any clams that are still closed.
Serve immediately, garnishing with fresh parsley.

 Discover more at *exploringmore.com/video/pasta*

TIRAMISU (CONTAINS RAW EGGS)

Serves 4–6

3 eggs
2 ½ oz (70g) superfine
   (caster) sugar
8.8 oz (250g)
   mascarpone
1 pack Italian sponge
   fingers (savoiardi)
2 tbsp Marsala wine
4 fl oz (120ml) espresso
2 tbsp cocoa
Dark chocolate, to
   garnish

1 Separate the eggs, then whisk the whites until they form stiff peaks and set aside. Add the sugar to the egg yolks, then whisk until light and frothy, and add the mascarpone, little by little, whisking constantly, until completely smooth.
2 Gently fold the whipped egg whites into the egg yolk and mascarpone mixture.
3 In a shallow dish, add the Marsala wine to the espresso and stir. Dip the sponge fingers into the liquid just until they start to darken, but don't leave them to get soaked through.
4 To assemble, place a layer of sponge fingers into the bottom of a serving dish, then spoon over about a third of the mascarpone mixture. Sift over a layer of cocoa. Repeat with another layer of sponge fingers and mascarpone. Finish with a dusting of cocoa.
5 Cover and refrigerate for a few hours. Before serving, garnish with shards of dark chocolate.

GREECE

With its glittering coastline and olive groves it's no surprise that seafood, olive oil and olives all feature heavily in Greek cuisine, as well as tomatoes and eggplants. Dishes can be simple – dips such as taramasalata or tzatziki, for example, or the Greek salad – or more involved, using filo pastry.

TRADITIONAL MOUSSAKA

Serves 4

Olive oil
1 lb (450g) minced lamb
1 tsp ground cinnamon
1 tsp ground ginger
1 tsp ground allspice
1 tsp cayenne pepper
1 large white onion,
  thinly sliced
1 red (bell) pepper
  peeled and chopped
2 cloves garlic, chopped
2 tbsp tomato paste
6 fl oz (170ml) red wine
1 tin (400g) chopped
  tomatoes in juice
2 tbsp fresh parsley
2 tbsp fresh oregano
2 tbsp honey
2 eggplants
  (aubergines), cut
  into ½ inch (1cm) slices

BÉCHAMEL SAUCE:

1 pint (475ml) milk
2 oz (55g) butter
2 oz (55g) all purpose
  (plain) flour
2 eggs, beaten
Nutmeg, grated

1 Heat a tablespoon of olive oil in a large pan and add the lamb. Sprinkle over the cinnamon, ginger, allspice and cayenne. Fry on a medium to high heat, until the meat has browned.

2 Discard any excess liquid. Then return the pan to the heat, add two tablespoons of oil and add the onion and chopped pepper. Cook until soft.

3 Add the garlic, cook for a minute, then add the tomato paste. Return the lamb to the pan, pour in the wine and simmer, stirring occasionally, until the wine has nearly evaporated.

4 Add the tinned tomatoes and simmer for about 30 minutes. Stir in the parsley, oregano and honey. Season, then remove from the heat.

5 To prepare the eggplant, add some olive oil to a large, shallow pan. Season the slices on both sides and then fry in batches until soft and light brown. Transfer to paper towels to drain.

6 For the béchamel sauce, melt the butter in a pan, stir in the flour and cook for a few seconds until pale and bubbling. Gradually whisk in the milk and simmer for five minutes until thick and smooth. Season with salt, pepper and nutmeg.

7 Remove the pan from the heat and quickly stir in the beaten egg. Cover the surface of the sauce with cling wrap to prevent a skin forming.

8 Preheat the oven to 350°F (175°C). Arrange half the aubergine slices in an ovenproof dish, then spoon over half the meat sauce. Repeat the layering process, then top with the béchamel sauce. Bake for 45 to 50 minutes until golden.

PORTUGAL

In its coastal cities, including Porto and
Lisbon, fresh seafood reigns supreme,
in particular *bacalhau* (salted cod stews)
and sardines. In the lush Douro Valley,
renowned for its wine, popular dishes
include roasted goat and wild boar stew.
Traditional breads are also fantastic.

PASTÉIS DE NATA

Makes roughly 12

8 ½ fl oz (250ml) milk
1 lemon, zest only
1 cinnamon stick
3 ½ oz (100g) superfine
(caster) sugar
2 tbsp all purpose
(plain) flour
2 ½ fl oz (75ml) water
3 large eggs, yolks only
11 ¼ oz (320g) all-butter
puff pastry

1 Preheat the oven to 475°F (245°C). Gently heat the milk with 2 to 3 strips of lemon zest and the cinnamon stick to a simmer, then remove the lemon and cinnamon.

2 Mix the flour with a little of the milk to form a smooth paste, then stir in the rest of the milk. Return to the heat, whisking constantly for a few minutes until thick.

3 Place the sugar and water in a saucepan, stirring until the sugar has dissolved. Bring to a boil and allow to boil for 3 minutes, then whisk into the milk mixture.

4 Place the egg yolks in a bowl and slowly add the milk mixture, whisking constantly. Transfer to a jug and allow to cool slightly.

5 Lightly butter all the holes in a 12-hole muffin tin. Roll the pastry out into a rough rectangle, then roll each rectangle up from the bottom to the top. Cut each roll into 12 discs. Place one disc flat into the base of each muffin hole, then, with wet thumbs, gently press out until the pastry comes about half way up each hole.

6 Pour the custard into the pastry cases, then bake for about 15 minutes, until set and caramelized. Sprinkle with sugar and cinnamon, then serve while still warm.

BACALHAU À BRÁS

Serves 4

1 lb (450g) dried salted
  cod
1 lb (450g) waxy
  potatoes
Olive oil
1 large white onion,
  halved, then thinly
  sliced
2 bay leaves
4 cloves garlic, crushed
2 tbsp fresh parsley,
  chopped
4 large eggs
1 oz (30g) black olives,
  pitted

TO GARNISH:

Dash of Tabasco
Lemon wedges

1 Cover the dried cod in cold water and allow to soak for approximately 48 hours, changing the water frequently.

2 Place the cod in a large pot and cover with water again. Boil for about 15 minutes, then drain. Allow to cool, then flake and set aside.

3 Peel the potatoes and cut into matchsticks. Add 1 to 2 tablespoons of olive oil to a non-stick pan and fry the potatoes in batches. Keep the cooked matchsticks warm in a low oven.

4 Add a further tablespoon of olive oil to the pan and add the bay leaves. Cook for 2 to 3 minutes, then add the garlic and onions to the pan. Sauté until translucent. Discard the bay leaves, then add in the parsley and the flaked cod.

5 Mix the eggs with a fork, then add to the pan. Keep stirring until the eggs are scrambled. Combine the fries with the cod mixture, then stir in the olives. Season to taste and finish with a dash of Tabasco. Garnish with lemon wedges.

(▶) Discover more at *exploringmore.com/video/bacalhau*

CARAMEL FLAN

Serves 8–10

FOR THE CARAMEL:

3 ½ oz (100g) sugar

2 tbsp water

FOR THE CUSTARD:

5 oz (140g) sugar

6 eggs

1 tsp vanilla extract

1 pint (475ml) whipping
cream

10 fl oz (300ml) milk

1 Preheat the oven to 300°F (150°C). Place the sugar and water in a saucepan over a medium heat. Cook without stirring, swirling the pan occasionally, until the caramel turns a deep golden brown.

2 Lightly oil individual metal molds or one baking tin, then carefully pour in the caramel, allowing it to run right to the edges. Take care as the liquid will be extremely hot.

3 Make the custard by whisking the eggs and sugar together in a bowl until light and frothy. Meanwhile, heat the cream and milk together in a saucepan over a low heat until steaming hot, but not boiling. Drizzle a little into the custard, whisking continuously, then slowly add the rest of the milk, whisking all the time.

4 Place the metal molds or baking tin into a large roasting pan. Add vanilla, then strain the custard into a jug, and gently pour over the caramel. Place the roasting pan in the oven, then carefully add boiling water around the molds or tin until it reaches halfway up the sides. Bake for an hour or until just set.

5 Allow to rest until the dessert reaches room temperature, then carefully turn out onto a serving plate.

 Discover more at *exploringmore.com/video/creme-brulee*

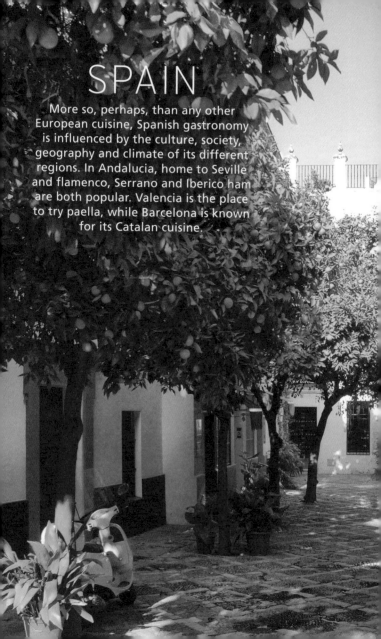

SPAIN

More so, perhaps, than any other European cuisine, Spanish gastronomy is influenced by the culture, society, geography and climate of its different regions. In Andalucia, home to Seville and flamenco, Serrano and Iberico ham are both popular. Valencia is the place to try paella, while Barcelona is known for its Catalan cuisine.

ALBÓNDIGAS CON TOMATE

Serves 4

9 oz (255g) minced beef
9 oz (255g) minced pork
1 Spanish (red) onion
2 cloves garlic, crushed
3 tbsp breadcrumbs
2 tbsp Cheddar cheese
2 tsp smoked sweet
  paprika
1 tbsp fresh oregano
1 egg
Salt and pepper

FOR THE SAUCE:

2 tbsp olive oil
1 Spanish (red) onion
2 cloves garlic, crushed
1 red chili, chopped
1 tbsp fresh basil
6 large tomatoes
1 tbsp balsamic vinegar
Salt and pepper
2 tbsp fresh parsley

FOR THE GARLIC
CROUTONS:

1 small baguette
2 oz (55g) butter
2 cloves garlic, crushed
1 tbsp fresh parsley

1 Preheat the oven to 350°F (175°C). To make the meatballs, combine the beef, pork, chopped onion, garlic, breadcrumbs, grated Cheddar cheese, paprika and oregano in a bowl together with the egg. Season generously.

2 With wet hands, shape the mixture into meatballs, weighing around 1 ¾ oz (50g) each. Refrigerate for half an hour.

3 Meanwhile, make the garlic croutons. Melt the butter in a saucepan and add the crushed garlic and chopped parsley. Cut the bread into cubes and toss the cubes in the butter mixture. Spread out on a baking tray and bake for 20 minutes or until crisp and golden. Keep warm until needed.

4 Next, heat the oil in a large frying pan and cook the meatballs in batches, turning frequently, until they have browned all over. Transfer to a baking tray and place in the oven for 10 minutes.

5 To make the sauce, add the onion to the pan and cook until just soft and translucent. Add the garlic, chili and basil and cook for 30 seconds, then add the chopped tomatoes and balsamic vinegar. Bring to the boil and season well with salt and plenty of black pepper.

6 Remove the meatballs from the oven and add them to the tomato sauce. Cover and simmer for 10 minutes. Serve with the garlic croutons.

CHURROS

Serves 4

8 fl oz (235ml) milk
2 oz (55g) butter
4 tbsp sugar
Pinch salt
9 oz (255g) all-purpose
  (plain) flour
3 eggs
Vegetable oil for deep
  frying

FOR THE CINNAMON
SUGAR:

2 ½ oz (70g) granulated
  sugar
2 tsp ground cinnamon

FOR THE CHOCOLATE
SAUCE:

8 ½ fl oz (250ml)
  whipping cream
9 oz (255g) dark
  chocolate, chopped
2 tbsp hazelnut (praline)
  paste

1 Place the milk, butter, sugar and salt in a
saucepan and bring to a simmer.
2 Add the flour to the pan and mix well to
combine, cooking gently and stirring until the
mixture forms a soft dough. Take the pan off the
heat and beat in the eggs.
3 Heat the oil in a deep fat fryer (or deep
saucepan) to 375°F (190°C). Test the
temperature with a small amount of dough.
4 Spoon the mixture into a piping bag with a
star-shaped nozzle and pipe the mixture carefully
into the hot oil, snipping each churro off with
a pair of scissors. Fry until golden brown, then
drain on paper towels. Toss the churros in the
cinnamon sugar while still hot.
5 For the chocolate sauce, heat the cream in a
small saucepan and then pour over the chopped
chocolate, stirring continuously until the sauce is
smooth. Stir in the hazelnut paste and serve
immediately with the churros.

PAELLA CATALUNYA

Serves 4

1 pinch saffron threads
2 pints (950ml) fish
  stock
2 tbsp olive oil
7 oz (200g) monkfish,
  cut into bite-size
  pieces
2 cloves garlic, crushed
1 large Spanish (red)
  onion, chopped
1 tsp paprika
2 red bell peppers,
  chopped and deseeded
9 oz (250g) paella rice
4 large fresh tomatoes,
  deseeded and chopped
5 oz (140g) frozen peas
1 lb (450g) squid,
  cleaned and sliced
9 oz (250g) mussels,
  scrubbed, beards
  removed
1 tsp salt
1 tsp pepper

TO GARNISH:

4 tbsp fresh parsley,
  chopped

1 Place the saffron threads into a large, wide, heavy-based pan over a medium heat and stir constantly until they just begin to give off their aroma. Add the stock and bring to the boil. Transfer to a saucepan, cover and set aside.

2 Return the pan to the heat and add 1 tbsp of oil. Add the monkfish and quickly fry until lightly browned. Remove the fish and set aside.

3 Add another tablespoon of oil to the pan. Add the garlic, onion and paprika and cook over a moderate heat for two minutes, stirring occasionally. Stir in the red peppers and cook until all the vegetables are soft but not brown.

4 Add the rice and stir well, ensuring all the grains are well coated. Bring the saffron-infused stock to simmering point and add half of it to the rice. Stir, and then bring to the boil. Lower the heat and simmer for five minutes or until almost all the liquid is absorbed.

5 Add the remaining stock, then stir in the tomatoes, peas and reserved monkfish pieces. Add the squid and simmer for five minutes. Arrange the mussels around the dish, pushing them into the rice. Simmer for a further 15 minutes or until the rice is tender and all the liquid has been absorbed. Season with salt and pepper. Remove the pan from the heat, cover with foil and leave to stand for five minutes. Discard any mussels that have not opened. Garnish generously with parsley before serving.

 Discover more at *exploringmore.com/video/tapas*

FRANCE

As you might expect, cheese and wine play a major part in all French cuisine, but each region has its own specialty. In Normandy dishes made with seafood, and apples are abundant; Provence and the Côte d'Azur are renowned for fresh vegetables, fruits and herbs; and in Burgundy, specialties include pike, perch, snails, game, redcurrants and blackcurrants.

BOUILLABAISSE TOULONNAISE

Serves 4

Olive oil
4 ½ oz (125g) fennel
2 red onions, chopped
1 tsp sea salt
1 tbsp tarragon, chopped
½ tsp black pepper
Fish bones and offcuts
2.2 lb (1kg) tomatoes,
   roughly chopped
2 tbsp tomato purée
1 pinch saffron threads
1 lemon, juiced
2 tbsp butter

FOR THE ROUILLE:

3 egg yolks
Salt and pepper
½ lemon, juiced
Pinch saffron
Pinch cayenne pepper
6 ¾ fl oz (200ml) olive oil
2 cloves garlic, crushed

7 oz (200g) salmon
7 oz (200g) pollock
7 oz (200g) monkfish
1 lb (450g) mussels,
   scrubbed, beards
   removed

1 To make the broth, heat 4 tablespoons of olive oil in a large pan over a medium heat. Slice the fennel and add it to the pan. Cook for 3 to 4 minutes without it coloring, then add the red onion, sea salt, tarragon and black pepper.
2 Add the fish bones and offcuts and the tomatoes, then cover with water. Bring to a simmer, skimming off any residue that rises to the surface. Add the tomato purée and saffron and bring back to a simmer. Cook for about 1 ½ hours, or until it has reduced by a third.
3 Sieve the broth, pressing down the contents of the sieve with a ladle to extract as much liquid as possible, then add the lemon juice and whisk in the butter. Check the seasoning, then cool and refrigerate until needed.
4 To make the *rouille*, whisk the egg yolks with the seasoning, lemon juice, saffron and cayenne pepper. Slowly add the oil in a thin stream, whisking continuously, then stir in the garlic. Add a little warm water if it's too thick. Set aside until needed.
5 Bring the reserved broth up to a simmer, then add all the fish. Poach until just tender, adding the firmest fillets first, then remove and place on a serving platter. Ladle over the broth. Serve with the *rouille* on the side and some garlic croutons or crusty bread.

BOEUF BOURGUIGNON

Serves 4

Olive oil
3 ½ oz (100g) bacon
  lardons
1 large white onion,
  sliced
2 tbsp all purpose
  (plain) flour
Salt and pepper
1.3 lb (600g) lean
  stewing steak
1 bottle (750ml)
  Burgundy or other
  good red wine
1 garlic clove, crushed
1 bouquet garni
6 oz (170g) button
  mushrooms
6 oz (170g) whole baby
  onions

1 Preheat the oven to 325°F (160°C). Heat two tablespoons of olive oil in a heavy casserole dish and fry the bacon lardons until golden brown. Remove from the pan and reserve. Repeat with the sliced onion, frying until soft.

2 Mix the flour together with a generous amount of salt and pepper and toss the steak well in the seasoned flour. Shake off the excess, then fry the steak in batches until well browned, adding more oil if needed.

3 Deglaze the pan with a glassful of red wine. Allow the liquid to bubble and scrape all the caramelized bits from the bottom of the pan. Return the bacon, onions and beef to the pan with the garlic and bouquet garni. Pour in the rest of the red wine. If the meat isn't completely covered, add a little beef stock or water.

4 Put on a lid and place the casserole in the oven. Cook for about 2 ½ hours.

5 About 30 minutes before the end of the cooking time, fry the baby onions and mushrooms until golden and add to the beef. Remove the bouquet garni before serving.

TARTE TATIN

Serves 6

3 ½ oz (100g) superfine
  (caster) sugar
2 oz (55g) butter
6 dessert apples
2 tbsp butter
11.2 oz (320g) all-butter
  puff pastry

1 Preheat the oven to 350°F (175°C). Heat the sugar and butter over a medium heat until it turns a deep golden brown. Don't allow the caramel to burn.

2 Peel and halve the apples, scooping out the seeds with a spoon. Place all the apples in the caramel and cook, moving them around in the caramel, for about 10 minutes. Next, in a 9 inch (23cm) diameter oven proof dish or pan, arrange the apple halves, rounded side down. Fill in any gaps with cut apples and dot with small pieces of butter.

3 Roll the pastry out into a circle, slightly larger than the pan and about 0.2 inch (5mm) thick. Place the disc of pastry over the caramelized apples, tucking the edges in all around the dish. Brush with melted butter.

4 Bake for around 30 to 40 minutes, or until the pastry is golden brown and the caramel is starting to ooze from the tart. Leave to cool for an hour before serving.

CROATIA

Formerly part of Yugoslavia, Croatia's location on the Adriatic Sea means that seafood is in abundance here, as are game and veal. Charcuterie is part of Croatian tradition. *Manistra na pome* – pasta with tomato sauce – is a staple and gnocchi is also a must-try.

GRILLED OYSTERS

Serves 4

16 fresh oysters, shucked

2 cloves garlic, crushed

Freshly ground black
  pepper

2 oz (55g) softened
  butter

TO GARNISH:

Lemon wedges

1 Preheat the grill to its hottest setting. Mash the garlic and pepper into the softened butter.

2 Arrange the oysters on a baking sheet, adding a teaspoon of seasoned butter to each one. Grill for five to six minutes or until the edges of the oysters start to puff up. Serve simply garnished with a wedge of lemon.

▶ Discover more at *exploringmore.com/video/oysters*

BLACK RISOTTO

Serves 4

1 lb (450g) cherry
   tomatoes
2 tbsp olive oil
2 cloves garlic, crushed
1 lb (450g) squid,
   prepared and sliced
2 tbsp olive oil
2 cloves garlic, finely
   chopped
2 ½ pints (1.2l) fish stock
2 tbsp butter
1 small onion, chopped
12 ½ oz (355g) Carnaroli
   risotto rice
5 fl oz (150ml) white
   wine
Salt and pepper
1 x 4g sachet squid ink

1 Prepare the cherry tomatoes. Blanch briefly in boiling water, then remove with a slotted spoon, peel and chop.

2 In a frying pan, heat the olive oil, then add the crushed garlic and the squid. Sauté really fast and remove from the pan as soon as the squid starts to curl. Reserve and keep warm.

3 In the same pan, add a further 2 tablespoons of olive oil and the chopped garlic. Briefly fry the garlic until golden and then add all of the chopped cherry tomatoes. Cook gently until reduced and thickened, then add in the squid. Season with salt and pepper, then keep warm.

4 For the risotto, heat the fish stock in a saucepan, then in a heavy-based pan melt the butter, add the onion and cook for 5 minutes until soft without coloring the onion. Add the rice and stir well, coating in the oil, then add the white wine and cook the rice until all the wine has been absorbed, stirring all the time.

5 Begin to add the warm fish stock, a ladle at a time, stirring the risotto constantly and never allowing it to dry out. Add the squid ink to the risotto and keep stirring, then keep adding the stock until the rice is just tender and the risotto is slightly runny. This should take approximately 15 minutes or so.

6 Serve the risotto and top with the squid in tomato sauce.

EGYPT

The rich and fertile Nile Valley and Delta is the key to many Egyptian recipes, which rely on legumes, vegetables and fruit. Pita bread and cheese also feature, and lamb and beef is often grilled. Fish and seafood are more prominent in coastal regions.

KOSHARI

Serves 4

2 tbsp olive oil

1 small onion, diced
   finely

2 cloves garlic, crushed

15 oz (425g) can of
   crushed tomatoes

1 tsp ground coriander

1 tsp ground cumin

Large pinch dried red
   chili flakes

1 tbsp red wine vinegar

Salt and pepper to taste

2 tbsp olive oil

5 ½ oz (155g) rice,
   rinsed

1 pint (475ml)
   vegetable stock

7 oz (200g) lentils,
   rinsed

7 oz (200g) macaroni

TO GARNISH:

2 large onions, finely
   sliced

Vegetable oil for frying

1 First, make the sauce. Heat the oil in a saucepan and add in the onion. Cook until softened, then add in the garlic, taking care not to burn it. Pour over the tomatoes, then stir in the spices and red wine vinegar. Cover and simmer for around 20 minutes, stirring occasionally. Season to taste.

2 Heat another 2 tbsp of oil in a saucepan, then add the rice and fry until coated in the oil. Pour over the vegetable stock. Bring to the boil, then cover and simmer for 15 to 20 minutes or until the rice is cooked through. Drain and reserve.

3 In another saucepan, cook the lentils according to the pack instructions until just tender. Rinse under cold water and return to the saucepan.

4 Cook the macaroni in plenty of boiling, salted water until *al dente*. Drain and set aside.

5 To make the crispy onion garnish, heat the oil in a heavy-based frying pan, then add in the onions. Fry until the onions are crispy and caramelized (this should take around 15 minutes). Drain on kitchen paper.

6 To serve, spoon the rice, lentils and macaroni into a large bowl. Spoon over the tomato sauce, then top with the crispy onions.

BASBOUSA

7 oz (200g) butter

12 oz (340g) coarse
semolina

3 oz (85g) all purpose
(plain) flour

1 tsp baking powder

3 ½ oz (100g)
desiccated coconut

7 oz (200g) superfine
(caster) sugar

7 oz (200g) thick
natural yogurt

1 tsp vanilla extract

TO GARNISH:

2-3 tbsp blanched
almonds

FOR THE SYRUP:

10 ½ oz (300g)
superfine (caster)
sugar

8 ½ fl oz (250ml) water

½ lemon, juiced

1 tsp rosewater

1 Preheat the oven to 375°F (190°C). Melt the butter in a small saucepan then set aside to cool.
2 Place the semolina into a bowl, then sift in the flour and baking powder. Add the coconut, and sugar, then stir in the yogurt, and cooled, melted butter to make a thick dough.
3 Butter a rectangular baking tin, then spread the mixture evenly with your hands, pressing down gently. Score diagonally and then again from the opposite corner to form diamonds. Then press an almond into the center of each diamond to decorate.
4 Bake for around 35 to 40 minutes or until golden brown.
5 To make the syrup, bring the sugar and water to the boil in a small saucepan, making sure all the sugar has dissolved. Turn down the heat and allow to simmer for about 5 minutes without stirring, then remove from the heat and add in the lemon juice and rosewater.

First published in Germany in 2018 by Viking

Copyright © Viking

ISBN 978-1-909968-33-2

Book design by The Chelsea Magazine Company Limited

Photography: James Murphy
Additional images: AWL Images, Getty Images, iStock, StockFood
Recipe testing: Rebecca Wiggins

Printed and bound in Germany by Mohn Media

vikingcruises.com